I AM Creating My Own Abundance

by
Barry Thomas Bechta

**UNCONDITIONAL
LOVE BOOKS**

*Redefining, Guiding, and Inspiring Humanity's
Connection to the Creative Power within.*

I AM Creating My Own Abundance
by
Barry Thomas Bechta

Library and Archives Canada Cataloguing in Publication

Bechta, Barry Thomas, 1968-
  I am creating my own abundance / by Barry
Thomas Bechta.

ISBN 978-0-9686835-4-5

  1. Self-realization--Religious aspects.
2. Spiritual life. I. Title.

BL65.W42B42 2009   204   C2009-905908-8

Publisher's Note
This publication is designed to provide accurate and authoritative information in regard to the subject matter covered. It is sold with the understanding that the author/publisher is not engaged in rendering psychological, legal, or other professional service. If advice or other assistance is required in those areas, the services of a competent professional should be sought.

I AM
Creating My
Own Abundance

I
AM
Abundance

Unless
I separate
myself with thoughts
from All Abundance

ACKNOWLEDGEMENTS

Thank You God.

Thank You Binah.

Thank You Anthony.

Thank You Zac.

Thank You Stephen, Margaret, Gabe, and Sam

Thank You Clare and Ellen.

Thank You Melinda, Paul, Sydney, and Gryphon.

Thank You Kimiko, Ernie, Inga, Walter, Uschi, and Peter

Thank You Sean, Brian, Anna, Sheyla, Chris, and Adam.

Thank You Virginie.

Thank You Esther and Jerry, Neale, Eckhart, Wayne, Louise, Mark, Robert, Jack, Alan, Louise, Richard, John and Jan, Michael, Sandra, Terry, Marc, Shakti, Lenedra, Ernest, Iyanla, Deepak, Jamie, Napoleon, Prince, Oprah, Anthony, Joe, Pat, Helen and Thetford, Brock and Wilma.

And most importantly THANK YOU for supporting me.

INTRODUCTION

Abundance is something that I have had very extreme experiences with. Thirty years ago I lived homeless on the streets of Dallas, Texas. Today I am building a new garage and new office to house my car and guitar collections.

From my Abundance perspective today, I realize that Abundance is always present. Even though Abundance is always present, you have to have a mindset of great money and Abundance in order to live a life full of great money and Abundance.

In my journey from apparent lack to apparent Abundance, I discovered that I held firmly to many unconscious beliefs that also held me to the level of Abundance I enjoyed (or not as was the case when I was homeless).

To transform my experience, I have used many tools to improve my beliefs about Abundance and this improved my experience with Abundance. I have written many books that talk about the transformation of my beliefs over the years including *Adventures Within, The Attractor Factor, Zero Limits, Expect Miracles,* and *Attract Money Now*. In fact, the last book in the list, *Attract Money Now*, I give away as a Digital Copy for free because I believe so firmly in my seven step formula to Attract Money, that I am sharing it with everyone who chooses to read it.

No person takes the same path to experience Abundance in their lives. That is the very reason there are so many books and processes and workshops in the human experience. The entire list of products and processes and experiences I have used to go from being homeless to being Abundant would astound most people.

In your hands you hold another Abundance tool. I believe the Divine inspired you to pick up this book today. Barry has a calm about him that infuses his work. He writes with an intention to create simple timeless concepts that empower people to Connect with God, rather than trying to change their outer world conditions.

I AM Creating My Own Abundance is a collection of affirmative self talk around Abundance. Barry's little book shows you that you have the power to choose the way you view the circumstances of your life concerning Abundance.

For most of my career, I've helped people understand how to improve their lives and live their dreams. During that time I've also encountered many people who are convinced that it won't work and that all those great and wonderful things that happen to others will never happen to them.

The world of self development seems inundated with the idea that positive thoughts will change you life. While that is a part of the solution, it is only one part. I believe that positive expectation coupled with action is the real key. You can try and convince yourself that you are happy, but if you mind is filled with counter intentions and self limiting beliefs that tell you otherwise, you will never make any progress. The only way to truly live your dreams is to clear away those counter intentions and take total responsibility for your own happiness.

Awareness is the first key to creation.

Attitude is the second key.

Action is the third key.

Barry's book is about all three of these keys: Awareness, Attitude, and Actions.

As you read the text, you may discover as I did, that it will encourage Awareness of the beliefs you hold that are both effective and ineffective. This is a good thing. This can be a subtle thing. You may read a line, and think to yourself, "That would never work for me." or "I don't believe that." That is your negative self talk working.

What if ... your Awareness helps you get more?

What if ... your affirmative Attitude improves your life?

What if ... your effective Actions transform your life?

What if ... you get one idea from this book that changes the way you view Abundance and more importantly your experience of Abundance forever?

That is my wish for you.

Expect Miracles!

---- **Dr. Joe Vitale**
Author of **The Attractor Factor, Zero Limits,**
Expect Miracles,*and* **Attract Money Now**
www.mrfire.com
www.attractmoneynow.com
www.miraclescoaching.com

TO THE READER

I AM the Feelings not the forms. When I wrote my first book, *I AM Creating My Own Experience*, I wrote a chapter on Abundance. A few years have passed since that time, and yet the Core of my beliefs concerning Abundance have remained constant.

Money is only one form of Abundance. Money is not the cause behind Abundance. The Feeling of God, The Presence within All That Is - is Abundance. Abundance is the Feeling of Completeness in every moment of Now.

The Feeling of Completeness results when you place your focus on The Feeling of God within you, over the forms you imagine your Abundance must take. In every moment of Now, The Feeling of God provides everything you need.

Everything you need is different from everything you want.

All your thoughts, feelings, words, and actions Create your reality. Your Abundance is recognized through your perception of Abundance. There is no right or wrong, good or bad, in your experience of Abundance, There is only your perception of it. You can perceive it in any way you Choose. It is always your Choice. Only you can make any choice about your life experience. Others may share their experience and ideas with you, however you Ultimately and Only Choose everything you experience about Abundance.

Being Abundant is a state of mind. At times, you may have felt extremely Abundant or extremely Absent from your Abundance for the same amount of money.

For example, when I was young boy, I received $10 allowance a week, however many things I wished to purchase or participate in cost more than my allowance. As a result, I felt absent from my Abundance. I also remember a time when I was a young man at University and I was scraping money together to eat and I received a unexpected letter in the mail from my Grandmother. In the letter was a crisp $10 bill, which I used to buy a bag of apples, a bag of bread, and some pasta. I felt extremely Abundant in that very moment. The amount of the Abundance was the exact same. The perception of that Abundance was totally different.

God, Life, Energy, the Universe (or whatever other term you use to call The All That Is), is Abundance. God constantly showers Love, Success, and Abundance onto All That Is.

Nature is constantly in touch with that Abundance.

Humans, on the other hand, get to choose their thoughts, feelings, words, and actions concerning Abundance, which can limit the flow.

The flow of Abundance in your life becomes very clear when you think about the last few times you were asked for money.

How did you feel?
What amount was your first instinct to give?
What amount did you finally give?

Whatever amount of money you gave mirrors your deepest heartfelt most secret beliefs about Abundance. What you believe creates your life experience.

When you say, **"I can afford it"**, yet you believe, **"I cannot afford it"**, it is time to ask yourself, **"How can I afford it?"**

Abundance is ever present. You can Choose anything concerning Abundance and God/Life/Energy Manifests your very experience as exactly that. You can see yourself as being Connected with all the Abundance you desire (or not).

Whatever your experience of Abundance is Right Now, that is exactly what you Believe you Deserve and are Worth through your deepest heartfelt most secret beliefs about Abundance.

This is not about blame. This is about Awareness. When you are completely Aware that you are totally responsible for your level of Abundance, you can truly look at what you have been Choosing up to now. Love everything about that experience, and you transform your experience.

Your transformation of Abundance only requires you to Activate an Awareness of the Abundance that is ever Present.

I wish you Awareness of your Ever Present Richest Blessings
Barry Thomas Bechta

TABLE OF CONTENTS

I AM EXISTENCE   Page 1

I AM OBSERVANCE   Page 5

I AM INDEPENDENCE   Page 9

I AM INNOCENCE   Page 13

I AM CONFIDENCE   Page 17

I AM MAGNIFICENCE   Page 21

I AM PERFORMANCE   Page 25

I AM PATIENCE   Page 29

I AM ACCEPTANCE   Page 33

I AM ABUNDANCE   Page 37

I AM REMINDERS

I AM GRATITUDE   Page 43

I AM ATTITUDE   Page 51

I AM TITHING   Page 59

Only
Now
Exists

I AM EXISTENCE

There is Only Love. There is Only Success. There is Only Abundance. Just because I AM alive, I AM One with this Love, Success, and Abundance. There is Only Love, Only Life, Only God. Anything other than Only Love, Only Life, Only God is a perception. A perception is a choice. A perception is illusory. A perception is anything other than The Feeling of God. The Feeling of God is Existence; Experience.

There is Only Experience or perception of experience. There is Only Abundance or perception of Abundance. I Choose what I believe in.

When I Choose to believe in anything other than Only The Feeling of God, I Choose to believe in everything other than Only The Feeling of God. Along with this choice, I Choose to believe in lack and limitation; I Choose to believe in right and wrong; I Choose to deny the very reality of Existence.

I make every Choice because I believe it gives me what I desire or protects me from something I fear. To Desire something means at some level I Believe I AM separate from The Feeling of God. To fear something means at some level I Believe I AM separate from The Feeling of God. This is a choice only I can make for myself.

There is Only Now. There is Only this moment. The past and the future are only my perception of the past and future. Now is the Only Time. This moment holds the key to this moment Only. This moment holds the key to healing in this moment Only. I may perceive that a past moment is being made Whole or Healed, however Only Now Exists. It is Only Now where Healing takes place. It is Only Now where Love, Success, and Abundance exist and can be experienced. Only Now Is Alive.

There is Only this moment. In this moment there is Only God. There is nothing else. When I Choose to perceive something other than God, I also Choose to experience something other than God.

When I believe that I must Choose something, I inherently believe I win with it or lose without it. I desire it or I fear it. This belief separates me from my experience of Only God. I AM Free to Choose what I believe.

I Can Choose Only God. I Can Choose Only Now. I Can Choose Only Love. I Can Choose Only Abundance. I Can Choose Only Success. I Can Choose Only God just for the experience of Only God.

I Can Choose what is Now Here. I Can Accept what is Now Here. I Can Love what is Now Here. It is always my Choice. I make this Choice Consciously and Freely.

There is Only God Now Here. If I perceive anything other than God Now Here, then I experience anything other than God Now Here. In my past, I have chosen to perceive many things other than The Feeling of God. With that choice I experienced many things other than The Pure Potential Feeling of God. When I choose Only The Feeling of God, I experience Only The Feeling of God.

I Choose Only God or I Choose something else. It is my Choice. It has been, is, and will always BE my Choice. I AM always at Choice. When I Choose to think, perceive, judge, imagine, or dream, I Choose to be and experience All in Existence. When I Choose to just BE, I Choose to BE Only God.

There is Only God. God allows for All in Existence. Only God Exists. I AM God. Being God is just as easy as being human. However being human involves struggle. That is the perception associated with being human. Being God is Only Now Here.

I AM EXISTENCE

I Can Choose Only God.

I Can Choose Only Now.

I Can Choose Only Love.

I Can Choose Only Success.

I Can Choose Only Abundance.

I Can Choose Only God just for
the experience of Only God.

Life and death are only
different experiences of God.

Gentleness and violence are only
different experiences of God.

Compassion and brutality are only
different experiences of God.

Peacefulness and hatefulness are only
different experiences of God.

Abundance and poverty are only
different experiences of God.

Positive and negative are only
different experiences of God.

There is Only God
or a Chosen Belief in God's absence.

I AM OBSERVANCE

I AM Existence. I AM God. God is All That is. God is Abundance. God is Always my Choice. When I Choose anything other than Only God, I can experience anything other than Only God.

God is Abundance. I AM Abundance. I Choose being-poor or Being-Abundant. It is always my Choice. Being-Abundant or being-poor is something I Choose to perceive. I Choose my experience of Abundance through my very observation of physical reality outside of me. I Can also Choose my experience of Abundance through my observation of the reality within me.

Do I Choose to see and claim with all my heart, mind, and being a belief in the illusions of lack, failure, and limitation around me? Or do I Choose to see and claim with all my Heart, Mind, and Being a Belief in the feelings of Love, Success, and Abundance within me? Do I Choose with all my Heart, Mind, and Being to Align with, Allow, and Accept God's Love, Success, and Abundance in my inner feeling world and outer form world?

Love, Success, and Abundance is All That Is. God is All That Is. There is nothing outside, beside, or other than God. God, Love, and Life are the process of God, Love, and Life. There is nothing other than this process. Now Here is Only God. Now Here is Only Love. Now Here is Only Life.

What about everything that seems to be other than Love, Life, and God? From the point of my ego (emotionally guided opinions) this can seem like a valid question. Yet this very question denies the existence of Only God, Love, and Life. There is Only God, Love, and Life, anything else is a self chosen limitation.

Since there is Only God, Love, and Life, all the things that seem to be different are illusions. There is no good or bad, right or wrong, there are only experiences of God/Life/Energy. Death, destruction, violence, brutality, hatefulness, poverty, and every other seeming negative experience are powerful illusions which appear through my belief in the absence of Only God, Love, and Life.

God/Life/Energy experiences God/Life/Energy through my

life experiences. God is like a temperature scale. On one end of the temperature scale there is freezing cold, while on the other end there is fusing hot. Cold or Hot are only different experiences of temperature. In actuality, cold does not exist. According to the laws of physics, what is considered cold is only a belief in the absence of heat. On the temperature scale, there is an experience of heat or an experience of the absence of heat (not cold - but the absence of heat).

Life and death are only different experiences of God. Construction and destruction are only different experiences of God. Gentleness and violence are only different experiences of God. Compassion and brutality are only different experiences of God. Peacefulness and hatefulness are only different experiences of God. Abundance and poverty are only different experiences of God. Positive and negative are only different experiences of God. There is Only God or a Chosen belief in God's absence.

In my past, it was the personalization of those different experiences of God, and my emotional reaction to those different experiences of God wherein I made up my mind that there was anything other than God.

Now Here there is Only God. In my inner world, there is Only what I focus upon. When I focus on Only God, Only God is present, and Only God is my experience. In my outer world, there is Only what I focus upon. When I focus upon Only God, Only God is present, and Only God is my experience. It is always my choice. I Choose whether I make Only God my focus always in all ways.

The Feeling of God is the stillness within my inner and outer worlds. The Feeling of God is without emotionally guided opinions. The Feeling of God is Calm and Whole and Complete. The Feeling of God is the space wherein all my thoughts, feelings, words, and actions take place. The Feeling of God is the Observing Presence within me.

When I AM The Feeling of God I AM the Observer of my experience. As the Observer, I AM in full control of all my thoughts, feelings, words, and actions. I may think, feel, talk, and act, however I Observe those from a place of Calm Gentleness. I

AM responsible for all the experiences in my life. I AM One with All That Is.

As the Observer, I AM Abundance. I AM Boundless. I AM Love, Life, and God. As the Observer, I recognise that Abundance is everywhere. I AM Extremely Abundant. Abundance is All There Is. Everywhere I AM is Abundant. There are birds and bees, trees and leaves, buildings and homes, buses and cars, people and places. There is so much Abundance. I AM Only Abundant.

In my past, when I believed I was absent from Abundance I was actually absent from my Observation of Abundance. Abundance is All That Is. Lack of abundance is only a perception I can Choose. There is more than enough for All That Is.

Now Here I have all I need to live Abundantly. There is nothing I require Right Now that has not been provided for me. I may imagine that I am without what I need. Now Here is there anything I truly need that I am without? I AM always provided for. I always have been, always AM, and always will be provided for.

God constantly provides All That Is in the same Loving, Successful, and Abundant nature. God can do nothing other than BE God. God is Love, Success, and Abundance. Within God, I AM able to Choose who and what I AM. God has given this ability to me, which allows me to fully experience All of God's Loving, Successful, and Abundant Being. My experience of Abundance is always my Choice.

When I Observe and Acknowledge the Miracle of Abundance in my life, it is all I experience in ever increasing amounts. When I Observe and Acknowledge the absence of Abundance in my life, it seems to be all I experience in ever increasing amounts. What I observe is what I Create. I AM Creating My Own Abundance. I focus on The Feeling of God, and God Creates the Perfect Forms in my life. I AM Existence.

I AM OBSERVANCE

God is In-Dependence of all that
I think, feel, say, and do.

All I think, feel, say, and do
Creates my experience.

My experience Allows God to experience
a part of All That Is through me.

My experience is Dependent on God.

I AM INDEPENDENCE

I AM Existence. I AM Observance. Love, Life, God, and Abundance are all the same. There is nothing else. The more I AM at One with All That Is, the more I AM All That Is.

In my past, I decided Independence meant to be separate from others in my experience. When I separated myself from others, I also separated myself from God. God is All That Is. God utilises All That Is as a mirror for me. Every person, place, thing, and experience is a mirror presented for me to recognise God/Life/Energy in All That Is.

Now, I understand that Independence means that I AM In-Dependence or Interdependent with All That Is. Everything I Create affects and is affected by everything else in Existence. My Independent actions are In-Dependence of All That Is.

God is In-Dependence of all that I think, feel, say, and do. All I think, feel, say, and do Creates my experience. My experience Allows God to experience a part of All That Is through me. My experience is Dependent on God.

Independence and In-Dependence form the duality of the human experience. I AM Free (Independence) to experience who and what I AM, through the Experiential Being of God (In-Dependence). When I Choose to be Independent or separate from All That Is, I Allow myself to deny all the Loving, Successful, and Abundant possibilities that are within God. When I Choose to BE In-Dependence always in all ways, I Allow myself to Access the fullness of God's Loving, Successful, and Abundant nature. It is always my Choice.

Being In-Dependence allows me to Enjoy Everything in experience, while Needing Nothing. God is All That Is. God Needs Nothing. God Enjoys Everything.

In my past, I struggled to be independent, yet I believed I needed particular people, places, and things to make my experience Abundant. Now, I surrender to my In-Dependence and I Enjoy Everything and Need Nothing to Be The Feeling of God Always in All Ways.

The voice of my ego (emotionally guided opinions)

screams that I MUST be, do, or have particular people, places, things, and experiences because I win with them or I lose without them. However, there is nothing I require.

The voice of God (Giving Ongoing Direction) within my life gently reminds me that I can be, do, or have particular people, places, things, and experiences just for the Enjoyment of them. No other reason. Perhaps at some future time, I no longer Choose to Enjoy them. There is nothing to worry about Right Here Right Now. All That Is, is Perfect.

When I Accept All That Is, God is Now Here. No matter what appears to be, All That Is, is God. I may Choose to perceive otherwise. It is always my Choice. If that Choice allows me to BE who and what I AM, I Choose it.

How are my Choices working for me so far? Do I feel Loved, Successful, and Abundant? When I feel the opposite, I can make different Choices just to Enjoy Everything. There is Nothing I Need. All is perfect. All is Whole and Complete. I AM All That Is. I AM Existence. I AM Observance.

I AM INDEPENDENCE

When I Accept All That Is,
God is Now Here.

No matter what appears to be,
All That Is, is God.

What I give is what I live.

Abundance is Everywhere.

I AM INNOCENCE

I AM Existence. I AM Observance. I AM Independence. I AM Humble. I AM Gentleness.

Life is For Giving rather than for getting. In my past, I desired to get many things. I believed life was for getting. I imagined Abundance was measured for getting many things in my life. I believed that all the things I got represented my Abundance.

Now Here I understand that life is For Giving. I AM All That Is and I Have all I need in life, I can give without affecting my Abundance.

The Voice of God within me says I can Give just For Giving. The voice of my ego says I Must Give just for getting. When I Give with expectation, the flow of Abundance decreases. When I Give without expectation, the flow of Abundance increases.

What I Give is what I Live. Abundance is everywhere. I AM Extremely Abundant. I AM Abundant in many things, most are Immaterial things. When I Give Abundantly from my Immaterial Being, I AM Being God. I Can Give Abundantly of my Immaterial thoughts, feelings, words, and actions to experience Extreme Abundance just For Giving my thoughts, feelings, words, and actions.

Giving and Sharing my Abundance allows me to express and experience The Feeling of God within me fully. When my Giving and Sharing has an agenda for getting, my experience of Being The Feeling of God decreases. When my Giving and Sharing has an agenda For Giving, my experience of Being The Feeling of God Increases.

God/Life/Energy Needs Nothing and Enjoys Everything. The Feeling of God Is All Abundance and Enjoys All Abundance. It is always my Choice to BE The Miracle of Abundance or the absence of Abundance. I AM always making a Choice.

Whenever I believe I AM without Abundance, I Choose to be absent from the reality of All That Is. There is Only Abundance. However I Can Choose to focus on absence of Abundance. When I make that Choice, it appears as if my Abundance is absent. Abundance is always ever present.

I Choose to Be Present. Now Here is All That Is. Now Here is Abundance. Now Here is God. Now Here I AM. The Feeling of God is Ever Present. I AM Ever Present. It is my Choice. I Consciously Make that Choice.

In my past, I Chose being absent over Being Present. Now I Choose to Be Present. Being Present is the same as Being Abundant. Being in the moment Now, is Being Abundant. Now everything to Be The Grandest Feeling of God is Present. I Can Choose to Be Present, Presents, Presence. It is always my Choice.

It may appear that other people, places, things, and experiences around me have made Choices on my behalf, but there is Only my Choice in each and every moment of Now. I Can concern myself with what I perceive around me, but that decision takes me away from the Choice at hand. It is always my Choice as to where I place my Attention. I may Choose to focus on God or on anything else. When I Choose anything else, I Choose to believe that something else has more power than God.

I AM Gentleness. I AM Humble. I AM Innocent. In my interactions with myself and with others around me it is always my Choice where I place intent on others and myself. The more Gentle, Humble, and Innocent I AM with others and myself, the more quickly my experience becomes One with Abundance.

In my past, I have Chosen to Be everything other than Gentleness, Humble, and Innocence, and my experiences have been less than Gentle, Humble, and Innocent. I forgive myself of my transgressions. I have Chosen to Forgive the transgressions I previously imagined others made against me.

There is Only God. There is Only Me. There is nothing else. I AM the Only One in the Universe. The entire Universe is orchestrated to provide me with the Perfect Opportunities to BE who and what I AM. I AM The Grandest Feeling of God, when I Choose to BE. It is Always my Choice. I AM Existence. I AM Observance. I AM Independence.

I AM INNOCENCE

The more Gentle, Humble, and Innocent I AM with others and myself, the more quickly my experience becomes One with Abundance.

Change is a Certainty.

When
I AM One
with The Feeling of God,
I AM Confident that what appears
to be is Only an appearance
that can Change.

Lack of Abundance is Only an appearance
that can Change too.

I AM CONFIDENCE

I AM Existence. I AM Observance. I AM Independence. I AM Innocence. I AM Certainty. I AM Joy and Gratitude.

Abundance is All There Is. This is a Certainty. I AM Confident that Abundance is a Certainty.

In my past, whenever I Claimed that I was Abundant, it seemed that everything opposite to what I Claimed came to pass. This was my perception.

Abundance is always there. I may Choose to be without Abundance. In my chosen absence of What Is, I am not. In my Presence of What Is, I AM. I AM Abundance when I AM Present with Abundance. Abundance waits for me to Be Present with it. Acceptance of Abundance in whatever form Present is the key to Allowing Lasting Abundance in my life.

Everything changes. Every person, place, thing, and experience changes. Life is Change. God is Change. Change is a Certainty. When I AM One with The Feeling of God, I AM Confident that what appears to be is Only an appearance that can Change. Lack of Abundance is Only an appearance that can Change too. Even lack of abundance is formed with Abundance.

When I focus on my place within The Being of God, when I access The Feeling of God, when I AM One with the Abundance of God, I AM One with All That Is. I AM All That Is Abundance too.

I Enjoy Everything no matter what appears to be. I Need Nothing. I Choose Consciously.

In the human experience, I Consciously Choose to Need Nothing and Enjoy Everything.

In the Spiritual Experience, I Consciously Choose Everything which empowers me to BE The Feeling of God.

I AM Grateful both when I experience Abundance and when I seem to experience lack of abundance. For I know with Confident Certainty that everything Changes. The most important thing that can Change is my Beliefs and perceptions about The Presence of Abundance in my life.

My Choice about Abundance Attracts my experience of

Abundance. What appears as a curse in one moment, can appear as a Miracle in another moment through my perception alone. My perception of All That Is Creates my experience of All That Is. I Choose everything I experience.

My Choice Can Be to recognise with Confidence that all Present conditions Change with Certainty. My Choice Can Be to recognise that being-poor in one moment Can Be replaced with Being-Abundance in the next moment. Or my Choice can be to recognise that All is Abundance, All is God, All is Life, All is Love, All is Change, and that All That Is present in my life reminds me to Align with, Allow, and Accept my Connection with All That Is in my life.

All my thoughts, feelings, words, and actions Create my experience of Abundance. I Can Choose to believe in the absence of Abundance. It is always my Choice. Only I Can Choose fear (feelings eroding away reality) to Be my experience of Abundance.

Only I Can Choose Faith (Feelings Automatically Inside my Truthful Heart) to Be my experience of Abundance. I Can Choose to BE Extremely Abundant with Confidence in all situations, no matter what appears to be.

Choosing to Be Abundance takes Faith. Choosing to Be Abundance takes Focus. Choosing to Be Abundance takes God/Life/Energy. When I Choose to Be One with God through Focus and Faith, that is exactly what I experience.

In my past, I Choose to Be One with human concepts of Abundance. I Imagined my possessions represented my Abundance: my bank account, my car, my home, etcetera. My possessions were Only Manifestations of God's Abundance through my deepest heartfelt most secret beliefs about Abundance in my life.

Now, I Never Overlook Whatsoever the Manifestations of God's Abundance in my life, and I Choose to Be One with God/Life/Energy (All That Is) Right Here Right Now. When I AM One with God/Life/Energy, I Confidently flow with All That Is and so does my Abundance.

Only I Can Choose my Confidence. Only I Can Claim my place within God/Life/Energy. Only I Can continue to make that

Choice no matter what appears to Be in my experience. I AM Existence. I AM Observance. I AM Independence. I AM Innocence.

I AM CONFIDENCE

When I AM
Pure of Heart. When I AM
One with God, Love, Life, Abundance, Health,
and Wealth, there is nothing I need or want to BE
other than The Feeling of God. To BE The Feeling
of God, I need Only BE The Magnificence of God
within. For what I AM within,
I AM Without.

I AM MAGNIFICENCE

I AM Existence. I AM Observance. I AM Independence. I AM Innocence. I AM Confidence. I Share All That Is Mine to Share. I AM Health and I AM Wealth. I AM Magnificently Blessed and Blessing.

I AM a human being, a human conduit for The Abundance of God. I AM a conduit for the Health and Wealth of God. There is Only Divine Health and Wealth in the Being of God. Varying degrees of Health and Wealth are accessible in the Being of God through my Choice and my Choice alone.

Within the human experience, All the Health and Wealth of God is at my disposal. Always in all ways the Health and Wealth I need is Present.

When I AM Pure of Heart. When I AM One with God, Love, Life, Abundance, Health, and Wealth, there is nothing I need or want to BE other than The Feeling of God. To BE The Feeling of God, I need Only BE The Magnificence of God within. For what I AM within, I AM Without.

The Magnificence of God is Ever Present. The Magnificence of God is Now Here. When I go within, I AM One with The Magnificence of God. When I take time to experience my Connection to The Magnificence of God, All That Is, is All There Is.

In my past, I went without. I believed that the only way to obtain Abundance was to pursue it in the outside world. This pursuit was futile in many cases, successful in a few, and a mystery many other times. The primary reason for my varying degrees of Health and Wealth resulted because in the heart of my human being I desperately desired more Health and Wealth or desperately feared losing my Health and Wealth. Both Choices denied the Absolute Magnificence of Health and Wealth.

Right Now, I recognise that Only when I AM One with The Magnificence of God within my inner world, do God and I become One in purpose. When I AM One with All That Is, I AM All That Is. I Can Only recognise this Wholeness through my Spiritual Being, not through my human being.

My human being tries to be, do, and have particular people, places, things, and experiences that equate to my human ideas of Abundance. My Spiritual Being IS Abundance within. Until I go within, I go without. I AM Abundance within The Being of God Right Now.

Of all the Abundance, I have experienced in my life, the greatest Abundance has been experienced through my Contemplation of The Feeling of God. Through going within, I Connect with the Abundance of The Feeling of God. God/Life/Energy's Abundance is Formless and Endless. The Feeling of God within is the Glorious place I AM when I fully Connect with The Feeling of God. All I AM is Formless and Endless and Manifests Magnificently into every Form and End I Choose. Pure Potential awaits my Conscious Choices.

Without God, Abundance is without my grasp.

With God, Abundance is within my grasp.

I AM God. I AM Abundance. I AM Love. I AM Life. I AM Health. I AM Wealth. I AM Form and Formlessness. I AM God and Godlessness. I AM.

When I AM. There is nothing else. There is Only The Peace, The Stillness of God. There is Only God. I AM God. There is absolutely nothing other than the Omnipresence of God/Life/Energy. There is Only Magnificence when I Choose to Believe and Access Only Magnificence.

I AM Existence. I AM Observance. I AM Independence. I AM Innocence. I AM Confidence.

I AM MAGNIFICENCE

When I AM.
There is nothing else.
There is Only The Peace, The Stillness of God.
There is Only God.
I AM God.
There is absolutely nothing other
than the omnipresence of God/ Life/ Energy.
There is Only Magnificence.
When I Choose to Believe
and Access Only Magnificence.

The Only thing separating me from particular forms
of Abundance are my particular beliefs.
My experience of Abundance Changes when I
Change my deepest heartfelt, most secret beliefs.
It is always my Choice.
I Choose being~poor or Being~Abundant.
I Choose being~pain, or Being~Joy.

I AM PERFORMANCE

I AM Existence. I AM Observance. I AM Independence. I AM Innocence. I AM Confidence. I AM Magnificence.

I work with my Abundance rather than working towards Abundance. Abundance Is. I AM. There is nothing I need to perform to experience Abundance. Abundance is a constant experience. Abundance is All That Is. There is nothing else.

My deepest heartfelt most secret beliefs about Abundance are what I experience. When I believe I must Perform certain actions to experience Abundance, I also believe I am separate from Abundance. When I believe I am separate from Abundance, that is the experience I Create. When I believe I Must, I generally act from a place of desperate desire or desperate fear, where I believe I win or lose through particular conditions.

I believe that Abundance is All That Is. I know that all forms of Abundance come to me in an easy and relaxed manner, in healthy and positive ways, for the good of All That Is. I experience The Abundance of God, channelled through my human being's deepest heartfelt most secret beliefs. Always in all ways I Create my own reality.

Performance is achieved through belief. Belief is achieved through Persistence of Faith. Faith is Created through my Choice. My Choice is Created through my Intentions. My Intentions inform my Choices, which Create my Faith, and through Persistence Create my Beliefs. All combine to ultimately Create my experience of Abundance.

The Only thing separating me from particular forms of Abundance are my particular beliefs. My experience of Abundance Changes when I Change my deepest heartfelt most secret beliefs. It is always my Choice. I Choose being-poor or Being-Abundant. I Choose being-pain, or Being-Joy.

To make a new Choice about who and what I AM in relationship to All That Is, is as easy or as hard a Choice to make as I decide. I AM Creating everything. I Choose hate or Love. I Choose poverty or Abundance. I Choose failure or Success. I Choose absolutely everything in my experience, no matter what appears to BE.

My deepest heartfelt most secret beliefs radiate from my being asking for everything that appears in my life to appear. God and I are One. God gives me the power to Create my entire experience. God gives me the power to deny my entire experience as well. God gives me the responsibility for absolutely everything in my experience, no matter what appears to be. Whether I Consciously Choose or unconsciously deny my experience, it is always my Choice to make. It is always my Choice.

What do I Choose Now Here? Since it is my Choice, do I Choose through being human or through Being God. Each Choice is valid, and each Choice carries different results. Every Choice is my Choice. I Can Choose it unconsciously or Consciously. God always Creates my Choices.

God always Manifests my deepest heartfelt most secret Beliefs. When I Choose something with doubt and irregularity, my Choices come into being with doubt and irregularity. When I Choose something with powerful Intentions and Persistence, my Choices Manifest with powerful Intentions and Persistence.

All Choices that Manifest in my life, Manifest for the Good of All That Is. There is Only God. There is Only Me. There is nothing else. I AM the Only One in the Universe. I AM the Only One in the room. Sometimes the Performance of my Choices seem to never come about, or they change and develop over the years, however no matter what appears to BE, Everything That Is, is for the good of All That Is.

I AM constantly at Choice. When I AM ready to Change my experience of All That Is, I make a different Choice about All That Is. I AM the Performer. I AM Existence. I AM Observance. I AM Independence. I AM Innocence. I AM Confidence. I AM Magnificence.

I AM PERFORMANCE

God always Creates
my deepest heartfelt most secret Beliefs.

When I Choose something
with doubt and irregularity,
my Choices come into being
with doubt and irregularity.

When I Choose something
with powerful Intentions and Persistence,
my Choices Manifest
with powerful Intentions and Persistence.

Right Now, my Choices keep me one step within loveliness and one step without loneliness.

I AM PATIENCE

I AM Existence. I AM Observance. I AM Independence. I AM Innocence. I AM Confidence. I AM Magnificence. I AM Performance.

Abundance is All That Is. Patience is a human experience. Only through being human do I experience the need for Patience. In Being God, All Is. In the experience of being human, all is not.

In my past, I have felt absent from abundance. I have cried when I imagined I was one step from the poor house, and I have become frustrated when I imagined I was steeped in loneliness. Yet, in my past, my Choices placed me simultaneously one step from the poor house and one step from the rich house.

It is always a matter of my perspective.

Now Here, I realize that Abundance is a Choice. Right Now, my Choices keep me one step within loveliness and one step without loneliness.

All experiences change. Every person, place, thing, and experience changes from moment to moment. Even something as seemingly permanent as a rock or a tree changes. Everything is God in Motion. Everything is Consciousness in Motion.

There is nothing that is motionless. All is in motion. Patience is motion. Patience is a Choice. With Patience everything happens in an easy and relaxed manner, in healthy and positive ways, for the good of All That Is. With Patience All That Is, is Now Here.

In my past, whenever I became impatient, I struggled in my experience. Whenever I fought against my experience, I fought against my Abundance. When I fight All That Is, I don't have a fighting chance. When I Love All There Is, I have a loving chance.

When I imagine that something other than All That Is, must be, I forget All That Is. All That Is Now Here.

Patience is an inner journey to an Awareness of my Oneness with All That Is. Patience in an inner journey of Acceptance to All That Is Now Here. Patience is found in the deep stillness of Being God.

Patience realizes there is Only Now. Patience understands

there is Only God. Patience remembers there is Only Abundance. Life is set up for me to win.

I AM Existence. I AM Observance. I AM Independence. I AM Innocence. I AM Confidence. I AM Magnificence. I AM Performance.

I AM PATIENCE

Patience is found in the deep stillness of Being God.

Being God is the Highest Level of being human.

At the lowest level, being human is based in fear,
lack, duality, and pain.

From the lowest level of being human, I can
transcend all my self-imposed limitations and reach
the Highest Level of Being God.

Being God is based on
Faith, Love, Unity, and Joy.

The Highest Level of Being God is something I
Can Accept as the basis to Create my experience.

I AM ACCEPTANCE

I AM Existence. I AM Observance. I AM Independence. I AM Innocence. I AM Confidence. I AM Magnificence. I AM Performance. I AM Patience.

All of Life is God. All of God is Abundance. All That Is, is Only God/Life/Energy. This is hard to understand when I perceive All That Is as less than Loving, Life-Affirming, Abundant, and Godliness. Acceptance is my path to Infinite Abundance.

Acceptance begins with Accepting All That Is. In my experience, All That Is, is Abundance. Even abundant lack is formed from Abundance. Abundance is All There Is.

In my past, I have witnessed the Miracle of Abundance and called it naught. I have laughed, cried, and been frustrated by the apparent lack of abundance outside of me. I have forgot that Abundance is my Choice to Accept.

I Can Only have an Abundance of Time for my pleasure activities by Creating a space of time for the activities I enjoy. I Can Only have an Abundance of Health by Creating a space for Health in my life. I Can Only have Abundance in All Its Forms by Creating a space for Abundance in All Its Forms within me.

Within my being I Create a space for my Abundance to germinate, nurture, grow, and finally manifest in the outer world. In the process of being human, there are uncertain time lines attached to Abundance. In the process of Being God, there is certainly time for everything. There are unrealistic time lines in the human mind. All is possible in the mind of God.

Abundance is cyclical in nature. When it appears I have more Abundance, I Accept that I Can share more at this time. When it appears I have abundant lack in my life, I Accept that it is time for me to Allow more Abundance to cycle in my life.

Being God is the Highest Level of being human. At the lowest level, being human is based in fear, lack, duality, and pain. From the lowest level of being human I Can transcend all my self-imposed limitations and reach the Highest Level of Being God. Being God is based on Faith, Love, Unity, and Joy. The Highest Level of Being God is something I Can Accept as the basis to

Create my experience.

Being God or being human are Only different vibrations on the scale of God. Being God is the Highest Level or Frequency of Light. Creation as God is Now Here. There is no time or distance to Abundance within God. Abundance is Now Here. Whereas being human can be at a lower level on the vibrational scale. Creation from the stand point of being human goes through time and space to reach Abundance.

Either, I AM being human or I AM Being God. I Can Only BE one or the other, until I AM All That Is. When I AM being human, I am being human. When I AM All That Is, I AM both.

I AM a spiritual being having a human experience. Through my human experience, I accept, reject, or select varying degrees of Abundance in my life. It is always my Choice. I Choose whether I AM Being-Abundant or being-poor. I AM the All That Is in my experience.

Until I Accept All That Is and recognise All The Abundance That Is Present, I shall continue to experience All I Choose to Believe. I Can Believe anything I Can Conceive. What do I Believe?

My deepest heartfelt most secret beliefs about All That Is Create my life. I Can Create haphazardly or Perfectly. Fear and doubt within, Create fear and doubt without. Faith and Focus within, Create Faith and Focus without.

To believe without a shadow of doubt is powerful. To Choose Faith Within is Powerful. The Power of God is Only one Choice away. I Accept that It is always My Choice.

I AM Existence. I AM Observance. I AM Independence. I AM Innocence. I AM Confidence. I AM Magnificence. I AM Performance. I AM Patience.

I AM ACCEPTANCE

*My deepest heartfelt most secret beliefs about
All That Is Create my life.*

I Can Create haphazardly or Perfectly.

*Fear and doubt within,
Create fear and doubt without.*

*Faith and Focus within,
Create Faith and Focus without.*

The concept of no choice is impossible.

Life is Choice. Life, God, Abundance, is
All That Is.

There is nothing else.

The concept of no choice is a part of all choices and
the result of that Choice is to deny my ability
to Choose my Oneness with God.

I AM ABUNDANCE

I AM Existence. I AM Observance. I AM Independence. I AM Innocence. I AM Confidence. I AM Magnificence. I AM Performance. I AM Patience. I AM Acceptance.

My outer world is a mirror of my inner world. Whatever my deepest heartfelt, most secret beliefs about All That Is comes into Being in my outer experience. Life, Love, God, and Abundance are only different words for the same thing. Life, Love, God, and Abundance are reality.

Always in all ways my Abundance mirrors my belief of Abundance in my Life. My level of Abundance in Health, Wealth, Relationships, World Experience, Peace, and Tranquillity is an exact picture of my beliefs in those areas. My Abundance results through my thoughts, feelings, words, and actions.

God showers Love, Success, and Abundance onto All That Is. That is God's Beingness. God is Only Love, Success, and Abundance. No matter what else appears to be, my entire experience is Only Love, Success, and Abundance.

What appears to be is only appearances, or Only God. My perception of what appears to be is always my Choice. Whatever I Choose to perceive, I Choose to believe, and I Choose to achieve. It is always my Choice. I AM the Only One at Choice in my experience.

In my past, it may have appeared that others seemed to influence me, or appeared that others forced me into a place of no choice, however it was always my choice to perceive, believe, and achieve anything. It is always my choice.

What I AM achieving Now Here, is my Choice. There is no other possibility. There is only my Choice. My Choice is constant and constantly changing. Every moment Now Here, provides another Choice. Every Choice allows me to Perceive, Believe, and Achieve something about who and what I AM.

I Can Perceive, Believe, and Achieve something through being human, or I Can Perceive, Believe, and Achieve something through Being God.

When I Achieve something through being human, I also

accept the framework that supports being human. The framework that supports being human, also supports lack, limitation, and fear. This framework also supports Love, Freedom, and Faith. The framework of being human is a contextual field that supports All That Is to Be all choices.

The concept of all choices is a being human experience. All choices suggests that there are different choices to make. Through the process of being human that is what I perceive, believe, and achieve.

The concept of no choice is impossible. Life is Choice. Life, God, Abundance, is All That Is. There is nothing else. The concept of no choice is a part of all choices and the result of that Choice is to deny my ability to Choose my Oneness with God. The opposite to all choices is One Choice.

There is Only One Choice to make. The One Choice is to Perceive, Believe, and Achieve Only God. There is Only God. There is Only The Love, Life, Abundance, Success, Health, and Freedom of God.

To Perceive, Believe, and Achieve Only God is powerful. When I look at my experience, what do I Perceive, Believe, and Achieve? Do I Perceive, Believe, and Achieve lack, limitation, fear, failure, sickness, or do I Perceive, Believe, and Achieve Only Love, Freedom, Faith, Success, and Health?

When I AM Honest with myself, I know I have experienced all choices in my past. Now Here, when I AM Focussed, I experience the One Choice, I experience Only God.

The most effective way for me to experience Only God comes through being out of my mind. When I AM in my mind, all my thoughts, feelings, words, and actions continue to support the contextual field of all choices and being human. When I AM out of my mind, I AM in my spirit, the Essence of God within me, wherein I think less, feel less, talk less, and act less from a human perspective.

Without unconscious thought, feeling, word, or action I AM One for the Good of All That Is. When I AM God, my One Choice compliments All That Is. My One Choice to BE God compliments God. Being God rather than being human is an empowering Choice of Being.

Being human includes absolutely everything conceivable within the human mind. Since all choices are conceivable in the human mind, all possibilities are perceivable, believable, and achievable. The human mind coupled with the Loving, Abundant, and Successful nature of God Creates all possibilities.

I AM powerful. I AM human. It is always my Choice.

The One Choice allows me to Perceive, Believe, and Achieve my experience in an incredibly powerful way. This incredibly powerful way allows me to BE All That Is. When I Perceive Only God and Believe in Only God, then I Achieve Only God. There is Only One Choice, Only God.

Making the Choice to BE Only God, allows me to Perceive, Believe, and Achieve Only God. My ego (emotionally guided opinions) screams that I give up all choices, when I Choose the One Choice. My ego screams that I lose my individuality of being human when I Choose Being God Only.

In my past, my ego did everything in its power. The only power my ego had, I gave it. Whatever I Perceived and Believed, I Achieved. When I Perceived and Believed in the voice of my ego, I Achieved it.

My deepest heartfelt most secret beliefs about Life always Manifest. Until I Change my deepest heartfelt most secret beliefs about Life, I stay at a similar level as I move through my experiences. Sometimes, my experience seems to blossom, then it seems to bloom, then it seems to whither, and finally my experience seems to die.

My deepest heartfelt most secret beliefs about Abundance always Manifest. It took many years for me to Change my Beliefs about Abundance. In my past, my Abundance was limited by the Abundance I could imagine I was worth. I thought, I was worth limitless Abundance. My results always display my deepest heartfelt most secret beliefs about my self worth.

In my past, I believed in just enough. There was just enough to Live. There was just enough for some things. There was just enough to be in debt. There was just enough to allow me to Choose from all choices. I Perceived, Believed, and Achieved just enough. Sometimes I even believed in big win falls, while other times I believed in struggle. All of it was always my Choice.

Now Here I Perceive, Believe, and Achieve One Choice: Only God, Only Abundance, Only Love, Only Success, Only Health, Only Freedom. These appear to Be many Choices, but they are words to describe All That Is.

This Choice is something that is made with Faith (Feelings Automatically Inside my Truthful Heart). There is Only Now Here. There in Only One Choice. There is Only God. There is Only Decision.

Abundance is a Decision. When I decide that Abundance is All That Is, I Perceive everything that seems to be other than Abundance as Only Abundance. When I Claim that I AM Abundant, the exact opposite comes to me. This experience of Abundance allows me to Choose my One Choice. When I experience Abundant lack, it reminds me to Choose my One Choice again and again.

There are many choices when I Choose being human.

There is One Choice when I Choose Being God.

This is only a Choice I can make for myself.

The Appearance of abundant lack is God/Life/Energy's way of reminding me to Choose One Choice, to Choose Only God, to Choose Only Abundance with All That Is. When I make that Choice with All my heart, mind, and being, then I AM. When I AM, I AM Abundance.

Abundance is the Only Choice Now Here with God. It is always my Choice to make. The voice of God Giving Ongoing Direction says I Can make this One Choice just for the experience of God in my life. I AM Existence. I AM Observance. I AM Independence. I AM Innocence. I AM Confidence. I AM Magnificence. I AM Performance. I AM Patience. I AM Acceptance.

I AM ABUNDANCE

There are many choices when I Choose being human.
There is One Choice when I Choose Being God.
This is only a Choice I can make for myself.

I AM Gratitude

No matter what consumes me, I can Let it Be
I can Choose to Fully Feel the Feelings within me
I can Love (with all my heart) whatever is
Now Here
There is nothing I need to do, but I can
release all my fears
My struggling inhibits
God's Life Giving Abundant flow
I AM the only one who can
stop my struggling and grow
God always says "Yes" to my dreams and
has no preferences
Only I can say "no" to
God Giving Ongoing Directions
So when I struggle, I can ask, "Where is my flow?"
There is no use worrying, Everything is Perfect
Let it Be what it is, that's how I Grow

Thank You God

I AM GRATITUDE

I AM Grateful for my ever increasing Connection with The Feeling of God within me. I Now recognise that God always says "Yes" to my dreams. I AM Grateful that I now recognise this truth.

I wrote the poem on the facing page as a simple reminder of the flow present in whatever is present in my life. Whatever is, is God Manifested Now Here. Only my thoughts, or rather my judgements, can decide that the present is unwanted, unhelpful, unworthy. So when something challenges me, I use this poem to remind me to find my Flow with God in my life. I wish to talk about the poem in a little more detail to fully explain the meaning within the words for me.

No matter what consumes me,
I can Let it Be

As I have opened my heart to express and experience my Oneness with God, I have been consumed by things that did not go the way I expected. I imagined that I had all the answers, that my way was the best way, and that I was without God when it did not go my way.

Now Here is the only time and place and experience. No matter what is occurring in my experience, God is providing me with everything I need to fulfill my deepest heartfelt most secret beliefs about Love, Life, God, Success and Abundance. God only puts into motion what I hold in my beliefs.

When something shows up and I believe that it cannot bring me to my dreams, I can either let it bother me, or let it Bless me. When I fight what I wish were not so, I invite and allow that experience to continue. When I Let it Be and look for the Blessing in disguise, I discover it and discover my flow.

When I am consumed, it usually has to do with my desire consuming me or my fear. My desire consumes me when I desire something to be in my life, which is not yet present. This desire can be for a person, place, thing, or experience. My desire will consume me to the point where I no longer allow the regular flow of God into my life.

Similarly my fear can consume me when I desire some person, place, thing, or experience to stay in my life the way it is. Desire and fear both can consume me.

Whereas Only God always Sustains me.

J can Choose to Fully Feel
the Feelings within me

I discover the Blessings in disguise when I Choose to Fully Feel the Feelings within me. The Feelings within me are many and varied depending on the circumstance. However the One Feeling that stays constant is The Feeling of God within me.

When something bothers me, I first Feel the Feelings of agitation or anger or frustration or disappointment. When I AM Conscious of my Feelings and not controlled by them I AM Aware. When I AM Aware of my Feelings I have also accessed The Feeling of God within me.

The Feeling of God is the calm, peaceful place within me. It is a Presence within me. When I AM The Feeling of God, I AM Calm and I AM Peaceful. I may also be Strong and Powerful, but within my actions there is a Calm and Peaceful Presence that directs my actions for the good of All That Is. This Presence watches over my experience without emotional attachments to particular results and allows the flow of What Is. When I Connect with this Presence within me, I allow the Flow as well.

J can Love (with all my heart)
whatever is Now Here

The Calm and Peaceful Presence of God Loves All That Is. When I Access The Feeling of God, I can Love with all my Heart, Soul, and Being whatever is Now Here. Whatever is Now Here, is the Perfect manifestation in my life.

There is Only God. I can Choose to separate my thoughts into many different illusions and beliefs, yet they rarely allow me to Love All That Is. When I AM One with The Feeling of God, I AM One with All That Is. No matter what appears to be, they are only appearances, perceptions, or beliefs that I Choose. I may Choose whatever I wish.

There is nothing I need to do, but I can release all my fears

There really is nothing I need to do in life. From time to time, I get caught up in the illusion of doing things. I imagine that I must do something to be a better person, or be a more spiritual person, or make money. There is nothing I MUST do.

God constantly pours Love, Success, and Abundance into everything in existence. Since we are all One. I AM Love, Success, and Abundance. There is nothing I need to DO to be provided with Love, Success, and Abundance.

Although that may be the reality of the Universe, I have Free Will. I may Choose to believe, perceive, and receive whatever I choose to experience myself as.

In my past, I Choose to experience this with fear, worry, and trepidation. My fears led to my struggle against whatever was present in my experience, and my struggle created my Life experience of struggle.

My struggling inhibits God's Life Giving Abundant flow

My struggle stops the flow of Abundance in my life. The Flow is constant. There is nothing that is not the flow. However, I can decide to focus on lack and limitation in any and all areas of my life and constrain the flow by my thoughts and my choices alone. I have the power to experience All That Is or to deny that experience. It is always my Choice.

I AM the only one who can stop my struggling and grow

I Can Choose to stop my struggling and grow. I AM Absolutely Responsible for my experience. All That Is experienced by me is All That Is allowed by me.

When I struggle, I allow less.

When I flow, I allow more.

God always says "Yes" to my dreams and has no preferences

God always says "Yes". No matter what my dreams are, God says "Yes" to them. God has no preferences about what I dream. I Can dream of lack, failure, and hate, or I Can dreams about Love, Success, and Abundance. I AM in control, consciously or unconsciously. It is my Choice.

Absolutely all my dreams are put into motion by God. In my past, many of my dreams were affected by fear, worry, and trepidation, while some of my dreams were affected by Faith, Confidence, and Tranquillity. Only with a Conscious awareness of my focus Can I accept the flow.

Only I can say "no" to God Giving Ongoing Directions

When my Awareness is unconscious, I regularly say 'no' to God Giving Ongoing Direction in my life. When I fight against what is in my life, I fight against God Giving Ongoing Direction as well. God always suggests the path that flows for me, rather than the one I fight for. When I Choose the path that Flows, I also Choose to express and experience who and what I AM fully.

Do I want to be right, or do I want to be happy? When I want to be right I fight with my experience. When I fight with my experience, I unconsciously deny God Giving Ongoing Direction in my life. What I fight against is God's Greatest Blessing in disguise. The only reason the Blessing is in disguise is because I am unconscious about it's purpose.

The purpose within the seeming denials in my life, is God saying, "There is an easier way." There is always an easier way when I let go of my need to be right and follows God/Life/Energy's Abundant flow.

So when I struggle, I can ask, "Where is my flow?" There is no use worrying, Everything is Perfect Let it Be what it is, that's how I Grow

When I AM Present with my experience, and when my experience is struggle, I can ask, "Where is my flow?" There is another path that is being provided. That path is not suggesting that I give up my responsibility. That path is suggesting that my greatest responsibility is to be Aware.

Awareness reminds me that there is no use worrying, everything is Perfect, and God is on my side. I Can Let whatever is Be what it is. When I access The Feeling of God, I open to the Blessing in What Is and grow in my flow with Love, Life, God, Success, and Abundance.

Thank You God

Thank You God. Thank You God. Thank You God. God always and resoundingly says "Yes". I AM Grateful for this knowledge and for my experience of God/Life/Energy. I AM

Grateful for everything including the times where I struggle and the times where I AM in the flow.

I AM GRATITUDE

God constantly pours Love, Success, and Abundance into everything in existence.

I AM Attitude

Until I go within, I go without
Until I have Faith, I have doubts
Until I love with all my heart, mind, and being
I miss the Presents The Feeling of God is seeing
My deepest heartfelt most secret beliefs
always come true
God's Love, Success, and Abundance
comes to me and you
Whatever I can Imagine
I can Be, Do, and Have
Whatever I believe comes to me, the good and bad
Whatever I yearn for, runs away from me
I AM Responsible for my life
I AM Responsible for me

Thank You God

I AM ATTITUDE

I AM Responsible for All that I experience. No matter what appears in my life, I have created it. God is Pure Limitless Potential. Everything is possible within the Experience of God. The Limitless Potential of God is accessed and actualized by all my thoughts, feelings, words, and actions.

Whatever I hold as truth within the core of my being, becomes my experience. Without a doubt, no matter what I believe becomes my experience of God in my life. I Experience the Limitless Potential of God in whatever way I Choose to experience the All That Is. I AM Absolutely Responsible for All That Is in my experience. This is God's promise to All That Is.

I wrote the poem on the previous page as a simple reminder that my Choices allow me to access whatever I Choose to experience. God always says "Yes" to whatever I Choose without doubt. Now I wish to talk about this poem in more detail to fully explain the meaning behind these words for me.

Until J go within, J go without

Within me, I have access to All That Is. I can experience All That Is only within me. Outside of me, I can only experience What Is Present in the moment. When I go within I access The Feeling of God, Giving Ongoing Direction in my life. When I go without I access the experience of ego (emotionally guided opinions) in my life.

Meditation is a journey within my being to Align with the Feeling of God constantly available within me. When I make a Conscious journey to access The Feeling of God, I access All That Is. I AM the Creator of my experience. All that I experience in my life reminds me that until I go within, I go without. When I look outside of myself for the source of All That Is, I go without the experience of All That Is.

All is Abundance. When I go within, I access and

harmonise with The Source of All Abundance. The Source of All Abundance is Limitless Potential. God is everything. God can be anything I Choose. When I go within and Connect with the Calm and Peaceful Certainty of God/Life/Energy, I know this, claim this, and experience this.

When I go without, I imagine I require particular forms to satisfy my definition of Abundance. My emotionally guided opinions remind me that I Must be, do, or have particular forms to be Whole and Complete.

I AM Whole and Complete Right Here Right Now. The only way I AM anything other than Whole and Complete is through whatever I Choose. I Can Choose to be hole and incomplete or Whole and Complete. Going within is a Choice that expresses my Core Attitude of Being Whole and Complete in my life. My inner life is the blueprint for my outer experience.

Until I have Faith,
I have doubts

When I AM Whole and Complete I have Faith (Feelings Automatically Inside my Truthful Heart). Only I can Choose my Faith as my Core Attitude. My deepest heartfelt most secret beliefs Create my experience of life.

Only one thing can be in my heart at one time. Either I have Faith, or I have doubts, or I flip flop from one to the other. Faith and doubt manifest in Limitless ways when I Choose one or the other. I Choose Faith.

Until I love with all my heart, mind, and being

My heart, mind, and being show to the world who and what I AM. The Heart, Mind, and Being of God are who and what I AM in the most essential form. When I AM Aware I Can Consciously Choose to express my essential form of God's Heart, Mind, and Being.

When I love with all my heart, mind, and being, I love all that makes up my essence. I love all my mistakes, my short falls, my shadows. All of the things about myself that work in my life, as well as all that does not work in my life make me who and what I AM. Until I love all of my heart, mind, and being, I restrict the flow of God's Love, Success, and Abundance in my life.

My heart can only access one thing at a time; doubt or Faith, fear or Love, failure or Success, lack or Abundance, denial or Acceptance. It is always my Choice what I wish to access with my heart, mind, and being. I AM the One who Chooses All That Is in my life. There is no other way for me to experience life other than through me. I Can Choose to access God first or last, Love first or last, Abundance first or last. It is always my Choice.

I miss the Presents The Feeling of God is seeing

Until I love with all my heart, mind, and being, particularly the parts I wish to deny, I miss the Presents The Feeling of God is seeing. The Feeling of God always provides me with the experience of whatever I believe in my deepest heartfelt most secret parts of my being.

I Can Choose what I wish to believe or I Can Choose from the Limitless Potential available to All That Is. I Can Choose Faith or doubt. It makes no difference to God what I Choose. It is only a Choice. With every Choice I make, God witnesses the All That Is through my experience.

In every moment, I Choose the best possible outcome I can imagine. When I love All That Is, I experience Whole and Complete experiences.

My deepest heartfelt most secret beliefs always come true

When I look back over my life, I can see the choices of my inner reality Manifesting as my outer experience. When I AM

Honest with myself about my experiences I see that I have Chosen All of Them.

In my past, some of my Choices were Conscious, while others were unconscious. The more Conscious I AM about my Choices in every moment of Now, the more I Consciously Experience who and what I AM.

God's Love, Success, and Abundance
comes to me and you

When all my thoughts, feelings, words, and actions come together to express the Faith of my Essential Being, All of God's Love, Abundance, and Success comes forth powerfully. The more clear my energy, the more clear my experience. The Love, Abundance, and Success to match my deepest heartfelt most secret beliefs comes to me always in all ways.

Whatever I can Imagine
I can Be, Do, and Have

Anything I can Imagine and claim with all my heart, mind, and being comes into my experience. When I Faithfully Imagine something with All the Heart, Mind, and Being of God it is instantaneous, no matter if I imagine something good (works for me) or bad (works against me).

In the human experience all starting places lead to my dreams. Life is set up for me to win. No matter where I AM, there is a path to my dreams along which I enjoy the Perfect People, Places, Things, and Experiences.

Whatever I believe comes to me, the good and bad

My Choices in every moment of Now Access the Limitless Pure Potential of God/Life/Energy to Create my experience. The stronger my Faith, the quicker the Manifestation.

In my past, there have been times it was easier to see bad experiences (working against me) as showing up instantaneously. When I recall being angry and in a fight with someone and found myself screaming "I AM fed up with this!", my thoughts, feelings, words, and actions held no doubt (they affirmed my Absolute Faith). My Choice in that moment Accessed the Limitless Potential of God to Allow my instantaneous experience of my Choice.

This principle works for me no matter what I Choose. More often than not, in my past, I unconsciously chose to fill my heart, mind, and being with doubts.

Now Here I Consciously Choose Absolute Faith in all of God's Love, Success, and Abundance.

Whatever I yearn for, runs away from me

Yearning for anything, means that I believe it is not currently in my experience. Whatever I believe is what I receive. Whenever I think desperately about what I wish for in my experience, I AM yearning. That becomes my deepest heartfelt most secret beliefs about What Is and Sets my Creation Vibration into Action to continue yearning.

I AM Responsible for my life
I AM Responsible for me

I AM Responsible for my life. I AM Responsible for me. I can only Create my experience. I AM only responsible for me.

There is no one else that I AM Responsible for.

My responsibilities may include anyone who is dependent upon me for support. My children are my responsibility only until they are mature enough to make independent decisions. My responsibility is to help them learn as quickly as possible the skills they need to be Aware in their experience, be Honest about their Choices in their experience, and be completely Responsible for themselves and themselves only in their experience. I powerfully share this wisdom by being Aware, Honest, and Responsible for my own experience.

I AM Responsible for me. There is no one who can take responsibility for me. Until I realize that I AM Absolutely Responsible for everything in my experience, the perceived good and bad, I rarely am capable of Creating my experience as powerfully as I desire.

When I AM Aware, Honest, and Responsible, I know my Attitude Creates my life experience exactly as I Consciously define.

I AM ATTITUDE

Anything I can Imagine and claim with all my heart, mind, and being comes into my experience.

I Tithe God Provides
God Provides I Tithe

I AM TITHING

God Provides absolutely everything in my life. I Choose the experiences of Love, Success, and Abundance I desire and God Provides them. God Provides for me without any effort on my part after I make my Choices. One of my Choices is to Tithe. Through Tithing, I Align with, Allow, and Accept the Source of All That Is in my life.

I Tithe God Provides

Tithing is the age old practice of giving back 10% in Gratitude for all received in life. In the past, many people tithed to a particular religious institution they were involved with. Today fewer and fewer people Choose organised religions for spiritual nourishment. Today people receive nourishment through many different avenues. All Spiritual nourishment ultimately comes from the One and Only Source: God.

Tithing is the simple practice of paying the Avenues of my spiritual nourishment a small percentage for all the good I receive. I pay my Tithe to the people through which I receive my greatest spiritual nourishment. Over the years, I have received spiritual nourishment through many sources including family, friends, authors, musicians, and people I only met on a single occasion. I Tithed directly to the Avenues of my spiritual nourishment and I have been rewarded immensely through God/Life/Energy.

Tithing is something I can Consciously pay up front or unconsciously pay up later. God, Love, and Life requires nothing of me. God is everything. On the one hand, God has no need for my Tithe. On the other hand, I benefit greatly through Tithing. The flow of All Love, Success, and Abundance in my life is Consciously sustained when I Consciously pay up front and Tithe for the Good I receive. This ability to Share my Abundance sets my Creation Vibration at feeling Abundant.

When I Choose to pay up front, I Consciously accept the part I play with God and acknowledge the Source of all my Good.

God Provides I Tithe

God is not punitive. God is Relative. God constantly provides Love, Success, and Abundance in my life. God also holds laws in place that make the Universe flow smoothly. God Provides and I Tithe. I Tithe and God Provides. It is a cyclical relationship that never ends.

In my past, whenever I Choose to forgo Tithing, somewhere at sometime, I had to pay for something unexpected. Whenever that happened, I Choose to play a victim and be mad (at God) for my loss. All That Is only follows the laws of the Universe. It is my Choice whether I Consciously pay up front or unconsciously pay up later. It is certainly easier and more Enjoyable to Consciously pay up front.

I AM TITHING

ABOUT THE AUTHOR

Barry Thomas Bechta is an artist, author, and film maker whose work centers around the concepts of Unconditional Love. Barry knew he wanted to write from a very young age and was encouraged with his artistic skills and only began writing full time in his thirties. He wrote his first book, *I AM Creating My Own Experience* as a personal journal to choose connection with God/Life/Energy. He has since written 17 inspirational spiritual books.

Barry loves to hear from people whom have connected with his writing and used it as a tool to improve their lives. If you would like to write him about your personal experiences as a result of reading any of his books, Barry encourages you to do so.

You can also get a Free Digital Copy of *I AM Creating My Own Experience - The Creation Vibration* from his main website:

www.unconditionallovebooks.com

Unconditional Love Books Titles of Related Interest
by Barry Thomas Bechta

I AM Creating My Own Experience
978-0-9813485-5-1
I AM Creating My Own Answers
978-0-9686835-1-4
I AM Creating My Own Dreams
978-0-9686835-2-1
I AM Creating My Own Relationships
978-0-9686835-3-8
I AM Creating My Own Abundance
978-0-9686835-4-5
I AM Creating My Own Success
978-0-9686835-5-2
I AM Creating My Own Happiness
978-0-9686835-6-9
I AM Creating My Own Experience - The Creation Vibration
978-0-9686835-7-6
I AM Creating My Own Experience - To Manifest Money
978-0-9686835-8-3
I AM Creating My Own Experience - 369 Conscious Days
978-0-9686835-9-0
Loving Oneness
978-0-9813485-0-6
Trust Life
978-0-9813485-1-3
I AM Creating My Own Financial Freedom - The Story
978-0-9813485-2-0
I AM Creating My Own Financial Freedom - The Lessons
978-0-9813485-3-7
Laughing Star's Guide to Laughter, Life, Love, and God
978-0-9813485-4-4

All of the above are books are available through your local bookstore, or they may be ordered as digital downloads at
www.unconditionallovebooks.com

Barry Thomas Bechta is available for interviews, special events, workshops, and lectures that redefine, guide, and inspire everyone's connection to the Creative Power within themselves. To arrange author interviews, special events, workshops, or lectures, please contact:

UNCONDITIONAL LOVE BOOKS

Unconditional Love Books
Box # 610 - 2527 Pine St.,
Vancouver, BC, Canada V6J 3E8

info@unconditionallovebooks.com

www.unconditionallovebooks.com

For additional copies of Barry's books, products, and services please contact your local book seller. Many products and services are Only available to order directly from the publisher as eProducts on the website.

Thanks for your purchase and Remember to Consciously Create your Life.

Right Now is the Only Moment of Creation

Enjoy it Fully!